How

FREE S   D

Download a pack of free support resources for Philosophy Circles, including all those **highlighted like this**, and receive ongoing support, by registering at:

www.thephilosophyman.com/circles

the
philosophy
man

"Philosophy is now on the weekly timetable and the children are really enjoying it. We will be sending out your philosophy questions for the children to try out with their parents. Thanks for all your support." - Janet Matthews

Published by:

The Philosophy Man Ltd
7 Tower Road, Writtle
Chelmsford, CM1 3NR, UK

Email: tom@thephilosophyman.com
Web: www.thephilosophyman.com
Tel: +44 (0) 1245 830123

© The Philosophy Man Ltd 2016

Contents

Miss Jones, this boy's book is empty. He hasn't written a word all year!

Don't worry, inspector. He's one of those naturally illiterate children. Runs in the family!

We never accept that a child is "naturally illiterate", however much they hate writing, because we know how much they would lose out. Yet we sometimes accept reluctance to speak as a fixed aspect of personality, even though a child who won't speak in front of their peers at school is unlikely to speak in front of their future colleagues. They may not get the same rewards for their learning - and their learning itself can suffer too.

Talking and Thinking Go Together
Speech is not just the result of thinking: it's where much of our thinking gets done. We discover what we think in talking with others, and others' responses help us think better.

Of course, some children are more introverted than others, but all children need to be able to access a speech-confident version of themselves. They also need to be able to challenge the views of others and demand evidence, not just for flourishing personal and work lives, but so that we don't get dragged to destruction by demagogues who thrive on ignorance and gullibility.

Not Another Thing To Do, But Another Way of Doing Things

Philosophy for Children (P4C) is proven to promote talking and thinking, with benefits for literacy and numeracy. In the "traditional" method of P4C, children respond to a thought-provoking stimulus by creating their own questions, voting for one, and then discussing it, with the teacher as facilitator.

This is a great model for committed schools once it is established. But novice classes often struggle at first to create questions that lead to satisfying discussions, and many schools do not find the time consistently each week for the full process.

Philosophy Circles adapts P4C for sessions as short as 30 minutes. These can stand alone, or seize the chance for philosophy within your own curriculum. You no longer need time for "something else". Instead, here is a philosophically rich, dialogical approach to what you already do, flexible enough to be used every week.

Ongoing Support

Resources highlighted in magenta are in the support download (see inside front cover). Curriculum-wide packs of resources can be purchased from our website for installation on your school network - over 160 session plans at the time of printing, with more added each term. You can also arrange for a Philosophy Circles trainer to visit for INSET, or to show the method working with your classes and then share the principles in twilight training.

Three Clear Principles to Structure a Change in Teaching

To make changes to the roles of teachers and pupils more secure, Philosophy Circles obsesses about 3 clear principles - Get Moving, Y-Questions and Take a Back Seat. See them at work in the description of a typical session, which is next.

A Typical Session

The children have been studying **Ancient Rome**. This session lets them think deeply about the genius and flaws of Roman society and themes still relevant today. First, the tables and chairs are pushed to sides to make room for a circle. You don't always have to do this – but the Circus Maximus demands a circle!

First, a **Get Moving** activity gets everyone engaged, talking and physically active. They imagine an all-against-all gladiatorial combat session. Volunteers model the weapons and garb of the competitors.

A metre ruler and a coat serve as the trident and net of the retiariius. Two shorter rulers are the swords of the diplomachus. The lid of a stacker box becomes the shield of a Thracian...

Which of these gladiators would be the last man standing? This is a **Y-Question** – one with reasonable arguments to be made on either side. More serious Y-Questions will emerge later in the session.

Just as the gladiators' different fighting styles created a balanced fight, questions where no side can easily land a knock-out blow make interesting discussions.

The children discuss for a minute, and then stand by the gladiator they think would be victorious (**Get Moving**). The teacher moves behind the clusters of supporters, so that as they give their reasons, they are talking to the other children, not to the teacher. Some of the children change their minds and move.

Now it's on to the deeper theme of the session: Why do people enjoy watching violent sport – gladiators for the Ancient Romans, boxing and martial arts for us? They provide possible answers that focus this open discussion into a **Y-Question**.

While they discuss in pairs, it's time for the teacher to **Take a Back Seat,** outside the circle, so that they focus on each other, not the teacher. Then a "pass-it-on" discussion begins, each speaker choosing the next.

The teacher sometimes asks for clarity, or volunteers relevant facts, but avoids putting his or her own ideas forward or leading the discussion. Some children think that if people wanted to compete in violent sports, it should be their choice; others think such things should not be on television because of the risk of younger children seeing it. They find their own **Y-Questions** within the discussion, inviting new concepts such as "maturity".

There are several comments about violent video games, and the teacher focuses them on a final **Y-Question** that has come from the group, not the teacher **(Take a Back Seat)**. Should parents allow children to play games with older age certificates? The session ends with a final **Get Moving** opportunity, with the children standing on one side or the other to show their views. Arguments ping-pong back and forth, and there is still a buzz of contention as they head off for break.

Get Moving

Overview

Think of children who are "playground confident but classroom shy". At break, they tell jokes, boss their friends around in games, give as good as they get in an argument. But inside your classroom, they're different. They might talk to a few friends at their table, but as soon as they know you're listening, the shutters come down. What is so different out on the playground?

They're standing up and moving about
Most of children's social talk takes place standing up – they don't generally go to dinner parties or sit about in the pub. The more movement there is, the more energy. Simply by having children stand up and face one another, you can make it more like talk for one another and less like talk for the teacher.

They don't have to speak to thirty people at once.
Everyone has a tipping point where one more person changes a group from "this is a chat" to "now I have an audience". Fewer pupils will close down if, especially at the start of sessions, you use not just pairs but small groups of gradually increasing size – and don't feel that every session has to build to whole-class talk.

They might be taking sides
Playful competition gives games purpose and energy. You are part of a team, with opponents to challenge. When children physically "take sides" in an argument, they feel supported by those who agree with them and energised by the responses of those who disagree.

There's lots of other noise

It's easier to avoid being self-conscious if you are just one part of a lot of noise and activity. On the playground, nobody is the centre of everyone's attention - unless there's a fight! Similarly, in the classroom, it's easier for reluctant speakers to talk if there are lots of other conversations happening at once. By starting with lots of voices in the room, you improve the chances that people will still be willing to talk in front of the whole group. If a reluctant speaker doesn't break their silence in a pair at the start, they probably won't when all eyes are on them.

Most importantly, out on the playground – you're not there!

Being aware of your presence is enough to shut down some children from talking, however supportive you are. We'll look at this in more detail in Take a Back Seat. The key thing for now is that for maximum engagement, talk activities that get children stood up, facing one another, with their self-consciousness lost in a hubbub of voices, are to be preferred to ones where they are sat side by side or at tables - especially at the start of a session. If you can get the children in a circle or other open space, great. If not, at least get them out of their seats. The rest of this section looks at how you can bring some of that playground energy into animated discussions.

Starting Positions

The popular image of the classroom of a "strong teacher" is of children quietly concentrating on their work. But when you want to shift to talk with everyone engaged, you want noise and energy, and quickly. Starting Positions is the fastest way to that.

1. Get everyone standing in pairs, with two clear "sides".
2. A fun, low-stakes question: give each side a side to argue.
3. Raise stakes - swap sides, bigger groups, harder questions.

Let's look at these stages in more detail.

1. Get everyone standing in pairs, with two clear "sides". If it's a long, thin space, stand in two lines facing each other. If in a circle, pair up and one in each pair steps forward and turns to face their partner. If sat in tables in rows, front and third rows face partners in the row behind. If sat at "carousel style" tables, turn to face the person next to you. In all cases, stand up, don't stay sat.

2. A Fun, Low-Stakes Question: Give Each Side A Side To Argue. Your warm-up question should be light, not require any specialist knowledge, and like any "Y-Question", be open to argument on either side. Crucially, it needs to have two clear possible answers, so that you can allocate one side in each pair to argue for it. The questions could be related to the themes of the session:

Inventions - Which was the best invention: televisions or computers?
Design – Which are better, spots or stripes?
Fair trade – If you could only keep one, chocolate or sweets?

Or if you don't want it to connect to the theme, perhaps because there's a surprise element to the stimulus, ridiculous questions that make pupils think creatively are excellent for loosening inhibitions:

Ask for two contrasting animals, and an occupation. Who would make a better teacher: giraffe or gorilla?
Ask for an animal and two modes of transport. How should an octopus travel: bicycle or train?

3. Raise Stakes - Swap Sides, Bigger Groups, Harder Questions. You can now increase the challenge by saying, "swap sides and argue the opposite", or have further rounds going from 2's to 4's to 8's, with questions of escalating toughness. For example:

Listening to music out loud, or with earphones? (2's)
Is stealing a DVD worse, or is illegal copying just as bad? (4's)
If most people think something is OK, does it make it right? (8's)

The aim is to move gradually from *"small talk"* in pairs on trivia to *"big talk"* in larger groups on serious matters. Children have more confidence to speak when their voices are lost in the noise of lots of simultaneous conversations. Then by raising the stakes slowly, you gently coax more children to whole class talk.

Other Examples of Question Sequences

If you are sequencing questions, mix it up so that one side does not get the easier side of every argument, or one side may get demoralised. If they are thematically connected, make sure each side gets to argue both ways.

Theme: *Rule-based Morality vs. Consequentialism*
Is it OK to lie to save someone's feelings? **(Y v N)**
Is it acceptable to kill to save lives? **(N v Y)**
Which is the more important ingredient in being a good person - following the rules or trying to make others happy? **(Y v N)**

Theme: *Reality*
Will video games ever be perfectly realistic?
Can you always tell when you are dreaming?
Can you be sure you are in the real world, and not a simulation?

"I was extremely cynical about P4C prior to today's experience... Watching the children transition from anarchic arguments about 'silly things' to thoughtful group discussion on a serious topic (the causes of poverty) was eye opening and quite staggering."

Adam, Year 4 Teacher

Theme: *Freedom*
Are pets free?
Are schoolchildren free?
Are parents free?

Why Allocate Sides And Not Just Let Them Choose?

P4C is ultimately about children making sense of the world in their own way, discovering and testing their own beliefs against those of others. So it might seem an artificial debating game to give them an opinion to argue for instead of letting them choose. But there will be plenty of time for them to say what they really think later, on matters of consequence. There are several advantages to starting with allocated positions to defend.

Participation: some children may be reluctant or slow to form an opinion. This is a quick exercise so by giving them a starting position to argue for, you go straight to the important business of giving reasons.

Disagreement: if one side of the argument is naturally stronger, both might agree quickly on it and then the warm-up has failed in its purpose of getting everyone talking energetically.

Challenge: having to argue against what you think, or for a point of view which you don't particularly endorse, is more challenging – you have to hunt for arguments instead of having them ready to hand.

Empathy: some children can be inflexible in their thinking, so having to come up with what someone else would say is good for extending their understanding of others.

Forming opinions: hearing reasons for both sides can also help in forming a more considered opinion about the question. You might ask them to stand to show what they really think, switching to a Thinkers' Game, the focus of the next section.

Thinkers' Games

Many figures of speech about thinking bring the abstract to life using physical terms: vote with your feet, opposing sides, stand in someone else's shoes. Activities that make thinking physical and visible to everyone are similarly engaging. Children especially enjoy these "Thinkers' Games" and they usually lift the level of energy and responsiveness in a discussion.

You can use them as one of your **Get Moving** strategies at the start of a session, or during a session to re-energise or to re-focus the discussion on a question that has arisen.

Think, Commit, Justify, Reflect
Most Thinkers' Games share this four-stage structure.

Think about a Y-Question where there are two (or more) plausible answers. Have some time to talk in pairs.

Commit physically to your answer. This is the stage that makes each game distinct, and which is key to it being effective. Move yourself, part of yourself, or some stuff, so everyone can see what you think.

Justify your answer with some reasons.

Reflect on what you hear, and show if you have changed your mind.

The Thinkers' Games minibook from this series details 38 such activities and goes into more depth about how to construct them. The key things are that the more movement and the more voices you have, the more energy there will be - and if it's getting out of hand you can take energy back out by having them sit down and talk one person at a time. Here are examples of the most popular.

Dividing Line
Think: Which is the more important to being a good person? Following rules or making others happy?
Commit: Stand over this side of the room for rules, over that side for making others happy.
Justify: Choose one child to speak first, they choose someone from the other side, and it ping-pongs back and forth.
Reflect: When anyone changes their mind, they can swap sides, or edge towards the middle.

Point of View
Think: Is it possible for a bad man to make a good king?
Commit:
  In an assembly - Hands on head for yes, arms folded for no.
  Sat at tables - Hands on table for yes, hands under table for no.
  Sat in a circle – Feet out for yes, feet under for no.
Justify: Look around for someone you disagree with, and try to persuade them to change their mind.
Reflect: Who's changed their mind and why?

Vote with Your Feet
Think: Which of your ideas is the fairest way to share out the lifeboat spaces on the **Titanic**?
Commit: Stand by the whiteboard with your preferred idea.
Justify: Tell them (other groups) why they should join you.
Reflect: If you change your mind, move to your new idea.

-Ometer
Think: Which of these cards is the naughtiest? (see below)
Commit: In groups, arrange them from most to least naughty.
Justify: Pair up with another group. Look at the differences in your orders and find out the reasons.
Reflect: If another group convinces you, change your order.

Not doing any work in school for a day

Hitting someone

Stealing food from the school canteen

Planning to make someone slip on a banana skin, but it not working

Calling another pupil a bad name

Calling a teacher a a bad name

Always Use Questions With Difficult Choices
More on suitable "Y-Questions" in Part II, but note that it's particularly important in Thinkers' Games that there is no obvious right answer. Nobody should be publicly caught out looking silly, and if everyone agrees, there's no discussion. I've dropped one of these **Naughtyometer** cards, because young children usually agreed quickly that it was the worst - can you guess which one?

You Get Far Fewer "I Dunnos" Using Thinkers' Games

The playful character, team feeling, freedom from getting the right answer and physical energy of the games mean that fewer children disengage or are reluctant to speak. Because thinking time is built in, and everyone has had a chance to rehearse their ideas, you can use whatever decision they have committed to as if they had put their hand up to speak, making the first response an ideal time to hear from a reluctant speaker.

You Can Create These Games Live, Using Their Ideas

As in the last example, you can capture their answers to a question during an enquiry, and then use them to create a game. This is particularly helpful as a way of helping you Take a Back Seat. Not only are the ideas coming from them rather than being pre-planned by you, but the quick phrase, "Tell them," redirects their attention away from you to the other children.

You Can Use Thinkers' Games At Any Point In A Session

They can change the tempo, add new energy, or focus on some emerging aspect of the discussion. They also become routines that you can use opportunistically in your wider teaching whenever a suitable question arises

You'll Notice People Find Ways of Breaking The Rules

It's fine if people put cards side by side, or sit with one foot in, one foot out, to show their answer is "a bit of both". I don't advertise the possibility in advance, but if someone wants to assert that they have a new shape for their thinking, that's all to the good. If everyone ends up with a foot either side of the line, you might have to declare that it is an "electric fence" and they have to get off to one side or the other.

Community Builders

"I watched how he listened. He listened badly. He is one of those people who do not really listen but are only waiting for their chance to speak. You can feel the talk machine revving in him; at best he is barely able to restrain it. And when he was no longer able to restrain it, the words came out as if the air had only been created for Trotsky to fill it with speech."

Richard Lourie, "The Autobiography of Joseph Stalin"

You may not have a Trotsky or Stalin in Year 4, but some of your pupils probably have habits that make it hard for them, or others, to participate well in a community of enquiry. Community Builders are activities that may or may not involve thinking, but which develop the particular skills a group needs to work well together. They can also provide a lively, motivating way to start a session and add variety.

Zoom in on what's difficult, and practice it in a fun way

After a few sessions, you will notice what they find challenging when working together in P4C, as a community of enquiry. The trick is to be as specific as you can, and choose an exercise that practices that skill intensely in a fun way. Fun cancels out fear, and practising without a difficult context will reduce intimidation.

You might have participants who are reluctant to be the focus of attention, or who hog the stage. Perhaps some respond with harsh negativity, or make points that are unconnected to what previous speakers have said...

For taking turns as the focus of attention - Mirroring
It's best if the players are in a circle, but any format where they can see each other is OK. Start as "leader", making slow gestures which the "followers" copy. Then point to someone else who becomes the new leader. They make some movements which the rest copy, and then pass on the leader role again. Lots of people get a turn, and it echoes the process of listening in which people take it in turns to speak and listen, be the focus of attention and give their attention to others.

For risk-taking and creativity - This Is Not a Spoon
Pass a large wooden spoon around the circle. The first person says (for example) "This is not a spoon, it's a tennis racquet" and mimes accordingly. The next person says, e.g. "This is not a tennis racquet, it's a guitar" etc., and the chain continues.

For building positively on others ideas – Yes, and...
All stand in a circle. In pairs, one partner says, "Let's..." and makes a suggestion about something to do e.g. "bake a cake". The other partner responds, "Yes and..." and adds a detail or extends the scenario "e.g. Yes, and let's make it really big". And so on back and forth, probably building into an extravagant scenario.

For eye contact - Eye Swap
Stand in a circle. Make eye contact with someone and then maintain the connection as you swap places with them.

For pursuing a chain of ideas – Philosophical Consequences
In a circle, start e.g. "If there were no schools, then all the children would run wild."; the "then" becomes the "if" for the next person, and so on round until you've gone all the way round the circle and can go from the first "if" direct to the last "then".

For giving justifications – Because I
The opposite of Philosophical Consequences. Start e.g. "I can't come to school tomorrow because I have been invited to see the Queen." Next person, "I've been invited to see the queen because I baked her an enormous cake." and so on.

Exploring problems – Why? Chain
Take a problem. the causes of which are to be explored. It can be large or small, real or imaginary. The person who proffers the problem is the first link in the chain, the question is, "Why?" and the next person stands behind them with a reason for the problem, and so on. Example:

"Lots of young people can't afford their own homes". Why?
"Because houses are very expensive". Why?
"Because there aren't enough houses," and so on.

Exploring solutions – How Chain
As with the "Why? Chain" but with solutions, not causes. Example:
"Poor people need to get richer". How?
"Help them save more." How?
"Give them better interest on their savings." How?
"Make banks give their highest interest rates to the people with the least money" and so on - this genius idea was from a Year 5.

For intense listening - Fingertrap

Stand in a circle with your right palm facing the ceiling, and your left index finger in the palm of your neighbour. On the click of my fingers, your goal is to trap the index finger of the person to your right, whilst releasing your finger from the palm of the person on your left. On second attempt, close your eyes.

For sharing talk fairly around the group – Pass the Thumb

This is helpful if you are using a signal such as a thumbs up to pass from one speaker to the next. Start by giving the signal towards the person on your left. They pass it on to the person on their left, and so on round. Then go back the other way. Third time, pass across the circle, making eye contact with someone and saying their name. Pass it round until everyone has been.

There are many other examples of community builders tackling particular issues such as listening, overcoming the fear of failure and so on at: **http://improvencyclopedia.org/**

Plan Your Own...

Starting Positions

Fill in your own set of Starting Positions questions, building the challenge but always with questions where you could argue either side. Start with the most serious and work back to the fun.

Topic / theme:

2's (fun warm-up question):

4's (more thoughtful question):

8's (something serious or challenging):

Plan Your Own...
Thinkers' Game

Create a 'Vote with Your Feet' activity in which they will stand in the corner of their preferred answer. Create a question and four possible answers which are equally appealing (or unappealing!)

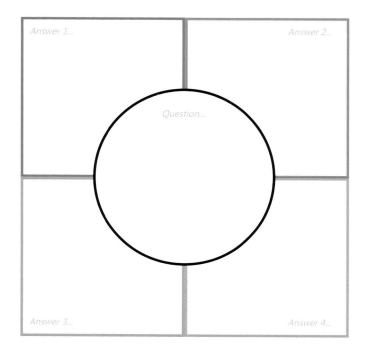

Answer 1...

Answer 2...

Question...

Answer 3...

Answer 4...

Get Moving

Summary

Bring playground confidence into the classroom

The more movement, the more energy

Use "sides" and disagreement

Not just for the start – use within enquiries and your wider teaching

The more voices, the more engagement

Starting Positions

1. Get everyone **standing in pairs**, with two clear "sides"

2. A fun, low-stakes question: give each side a side to argue

3. Raise stakes: swap sides, bigger groups, harder questions

Thinkers' Games

Think about a Y-Question

Commit physically to your answer (move yourself, part of yourself, or some stuff)

Justify your answer with some reasons

Reflect on what you hear, and show if you change your mind

Community Builders

What do they find **difficult**?

Zoom in on exactly what the skill needed is

Find a way to **practice** it repeatedly that is fun

Y-Questions

Overview

Two roads diverged in a yellow wood,
And sorry I could not travel both
And be one traveler, long I stood
And looked down one as far as I could
To where it bent in the undergrowth;

Then took the other, as just as fair,
And having perhaps the better claim,
Because it was grassy and wanted wear;
Though as for that the passing there
Had worn them really about the same,

And both that morning equally lay
In leaves no step had trodden black.
Oh, I kept the first for another day!
Yet knowing how way leads on to way,
I doubted if I should ever come back.

I shall be telling this with a sigh
Somewhere ages and ages hence:
Two roads diverged in a wood, and I—
I took the one less traveled by,
And that has made all the difference.

Robert Frost, The Road Not Taken (1916)

The Robert Frost poem illustrates the desired effect of a "Y-Question". A question that presents a decision between two diverging answers, each equally appealing, makes it very difficult to choose between them. When it seems that perhaps one side has the better claim, there is a counterargument for the other side. The harder it is to choose, the deeper the argument can go.

Note that this isn't the same as saying "there are no right or wrong answers in philosophy". Which questions are open to definitive right answers is a philosophical question of its own. However, children do feel empowered to say what they think, rather that what they think you want them to say. It becomes easier for them to look to one another for answers instead of waiting for your feedback. It's transformative for children who normally struggle to find the answers the teacher wants.

Why use closed questions, not open ones?
"Can it ever be wrong to forgive someone?" is "closed", because there are only two choices - in this case, "yes" or "no". That means focus is provided at the outset by the question, allowing the facilitator to Take a Back Seat. The discussion will be responsive and dialogical because the participants are arguing about the same thing. For some questions, especially if using a Thinkers' Game, it can work well to have three or four options.

Turn Open Questions into Y-Questions
"Why is forgiveness important?" is an "open" question, because any number of answers could fit it. It might lead thoughtful talk with many different answers, but will tend towards isolated points and little challenge because the discussion is not contained.

The best approach with such open questions is to get the children to turn them into Y-Questions. Have an answer-creating phase to gather three or four distinct, plausible proposals. After that, the discussion turns to critical thinking, testing only the answers already given against evidence and examples, just as it would if you had started with a Y-Question. This deliberate focus gives you a chance to make progress before you run out of time.

Not all Y-Questions are Philosophical

That there are arguments on either side is not by itself, enough to make a Y-Question philosophical. As well as being hard to decide, the best Y-Questions involve important concepts that are hard to define. The questions in the inside front cover give examples of philosophical conflicts of opinion that do matter – about values, knowledge, politics, reality, reasoning.

Please don't think that you are doing philosophy if you simply throw a series of, "Would you rather?" questions at children. It's a way of getting them ready to do philosophy, but isn't "the thing itself". That said, carefully chosen and facilitated questions, such as this one in the Spot & Stripe series for younger children, can have important ideas lurking just below the surface.

"Would you rather be a king or a wizard?"

A starting point for talking about power and responsibility.

Stimuli

1. Is it acceptable to save five lives at the cost of one?

2. A group of six are exploring a cave. It floods, blocking all exits but one. Eric rushes ahead. His gets his head out into the fresh air, but gets wedged. They pull and push; he won't budge. But they do have some high explosive, just enough to blow Eric up but not enough to blast a new exit. Is it OK for them to blow Eric up to save themselves? If they don't, they will drown as the waters rise, while Eric will survive and eventually be rescued.

A Stimulus Can Bring a Question to Life

Just asking a question can sometimes be enough to start a lively discussion. But a stimulus that gives a context for the discussion makes it more engaging, especially if it involves characters and dilemmas. Many of the questions philosophy deals with are general and abstract. A stimulus gives children something more concrete to focus on to begin with, and more general principles can be uncovered as the discussion progresses.

It Should Tell You What to Think About, Not What to Think

You may have heard "The Parable of the Long Spoons". A visitor to hell and heaven sees the damned and the saved sat at separate sumptuous banquets - equipped with four-foot long spoons. The only difference is that the damned are trying to feed themselves, and starving because they cannot reach their mouths, while the saved are joyfully feeding each other. The message, loud and clear, is "It's good to share". Compare that preachy message with the story opposite.

Someone walked up to Frizz and Shine and asked Shine, "Will you be my friend?"

"No thanks," said Frizz. "Shine already has a friend." Someone walked away.

"I might have liked another friend," said Shine. "Then I would have had two."

"Yes," said Frizz.
"But I would only have a half."

From Frizz and Shine by Jason Buckley & Steve Williams.
Available on www.p4c.com

When you want to get children thinking for themselves, don't make life harder by starting with something that tells them what to think, or you will get a shallow recitation of what they think you want to hear. Your role here is to facilitate, not to teach, still less to preach. So seek out things that are ambiguous, problematic, conflicted, provocative, puzzling, complex, - but not sugary, unless there is some salt with the sugar.

Using the Frizz and Shine story as a stimulus, you could ask, "If you have to share a friend, do you get less of them?", or get the children to create their own questions. The concepts of friendship, jealousy, sharing are all in play, but the stimulus presents conflicting views without endorsing one or the other.

Unfinished Business
A common difficulty with using established stories as stimuli is that they usually have an ending or moral that settles things. Instead, find a moment in a story when a decision has to be taken, or a point in a dialogue that has not reached a conclusion. The discussion can then carry on where the situation leaves off. Stories and dialogues that are written specifically for P4C will often deliberately be "unfinished business" so that the stimulus asks or invites questions, but does not provide a final answer to them.

Finding Stimuli
What you are always looking for is something that brings to the surface a concept about which people can disagree. Abstract nouns that come in opposites are a rich source of philosophically interesting concepts: fairness and unfairness, happiness and unhappiness, reality and appearance, power and weakness.

Stimuli Are Everywhere

Video clips, news stories, pictures and objects can also make excellent stimuli. Four of the most common ways that stimuli raise such concepts for discussion, along with examples from the support download or elsewhere are:

Exaggerate: pursue a concept to an extreme ("**The Fairest Teacher of Them All**", video clip "Killing Time with Friends").

Clash: in which two opposing values clash ("**The Dog and the Fox**", painting "An Experiment on a Bird in an Air Pump").

Reverse: invert the ordinary order of things ("**Toys for the Boys**", picture book "I Want to be A Cowgirl").

Remove: remove something from the world and see what happens ("**The Numbers Strike**", film "The Invention of Lying").

Experiences as Stimuli

Actively doing, rather than viewing or reading, is a very powerful stimulus. I often use the "Human Knot" in which participants join hands with one another and then have to untangle themselves. It raises many questions about leadership, cooperation and persistence.

Philosophy in Role

"Right, me hearties. We've found the gold! We're rich!"

"Arrr!"

"Or at least, I'm rich, and you're going to be a bit less poor. As it's my ship, I get half the treasure. You can form a pirate council to decide how to share out the other half. Bear in mind that some of you have been on the boat for years, but others have only just joined and aren't much use yet. I'll leave it to you."

Taking a decision as participants inside a story about pirates is a lot more engaging than answering, "How should rewards be shared between labour and capital?" It becomes urgent and specific, and the children can move between the pirate and the real world.

Be Prepared to Welcome a Mutiny!
On one occasion, a chant of, "All get the same!" started in Year 4 and spread through a whole assembly hall.

I was deposed as captain, and the discussion shifted to how to choose a new leader. It's this ability for the narrative to propel the discussion that makes this way of doing P4C especially exciting. Because it's their story, it's their discussion too. If you can respond to where they want to take the story, while building in new opportunities for deeper thinking, it's a joy all round.

It Helps If Their Roles Have Conflict Built In
For example, half the class are peasants who want to clear a forest for cash crops to pay for their children's education, half are conservationists seeking to preserve a rare habitat.

They Can Step Back Out of Role At the End
This can be a helpful move in taking the discussion to a more general level of universal principles. In the example above, you might return them to their normal selves and they can talk from a neutral perspective, having extended their thinking in-role.

You Only Need the Thinnest Wrapper of a Story
Most questions can be approached this way. The "fat caver" story earlier, or other thought experiments from academic philosophy, work well if the children are in the story taking the decision. Or insert your question into a "Lord of the Flies" scenario where decisions must be taken without adults. There are also Philosophy in Role opportunities within your existing curriculum - the topic of the next section.

Philosophy in Your Curriculum

The curriculum is crowded. A typical week in a UK primary school squeezes in creative subjects, humanities, and PE around maths, literacy, and an ever-changing government initiative alphabet soup of SEAL, SMSC, PSHE and PVE. It's understandable to worry that philosophy is yet another thing to do.

Philosophy Circles can be used within the existing curriculum. There are opportunities for philosophy in every discipline - from maths, to history, to science. In general, a subject that doesn't raise philosophical questions is probably not worth studying!

Of course, there's no doubt that schools that set time aside for a stand-alone P4C session see the benefits. There is something particularly precious about classes and teachers who choose together what to explore in philosophy. But whether as a bridge to that, as an addition to it, or as the best that can be done under the pressure, planning these sessions into your curriculum gives more children more opportunities to enjoy this way of thinking.

Start With Three Concepts
To find the philosophy in a topic or text you are studying, you need to step away from the content at first and then come back to it. Start with concepts, not content. So with the Romans, for example, don't think, "55 BC" or "Roman baths". What are the big ideas of universal human importance that are relevant to this topic? Again, abstract nouns that come in opposites are a good way in, as are emotions, and things that connect to status or value judgments. Roles or types of people also work. Sticking to three concepts and using a table seems to be best.

Next, Three Questions, Then Three Stimuli

For each of the concepts you have chosen, create a Y-Question that you can ask in the context of the topic or text. Remember it needs to be hard to decide what your answer is. Then consider a stimulus or area to learn about that will set up the question.

CONCEPT	Cruelty	Imperial vs. Republic	Men/Women
QUESTION	Why do we/ Romans enjoy violent sports?	Which was better: the Republic or the Empire?	Would you rather have been a Patrician woman or a Plebian man?
STIMULUS	**Ancient Rome gladiators**	Maps of Republic and Empire, snippets from historians and speeches.	Daily lives and the laws that determined what different classes and genders did.

Notice that the discussions are intimately connected to the factual learning about the topic. What they learn helps them give more informed answers, and the deeper questions motivate the learning. The philosophical aspect is that wider values such as freedom, compassion, equality, autonomy are involved: they are talking about Ancient Rome, but in doing so they are discussing issues of permanent human importance.

Plan Your Own...

Y-Questions

Create a set of juicy, balanced Y-Questions by using these question stems and the concepts at the bottom (or any of your own). The harder the better!

Is...

Does...

Should...

Fairness/Equality   Reality/Illusion   Progress/Tradition

Co-create some Y-Questions, where you create the question and the children propose three or four answers, before focusing the discussion on which answer is most plausible.

Why...

Which...

When...

Strength/Weakness Morality/Law Freedom/Obedience

Y-Questions

Summary

Find questions with arguments on both sides

Look for hard-to-define, important concepts

Specific questions that raise general concepts are powerful

Closed questions can focus the argument

The harder the choice, the deeper the thinking

Stimuli

When you can, devise an experience that can provide a stimulus

Find things that exaggerate, clash, reverse, or remove concepts

Give them a thing to think about, don't tell them what to think

---

Philosophy in Role

Put the participants inside the story, facing a dilemma

Build in conflict between rival groups if you can

Be willing to play and follow the story where they take it

Philosophy in Your Curriculum

Step away from content, then come back to it

Work from concepts to questions to stimuli

Use concepts important in the wider world as well as the topic

Take a Back Seat

Overview

Have You Ever Seen Young Children "Playing Schools"?
What's the time of day they most often act out? Almost
everyone says it's the register. My nieces used to come in from
a hard day at school, line up their dolls and register them within
an inch of their lives. The dolls never learned anything, but they
certainly wouldn't have dared to bunk off.

Why is the Register the Time Children Choose to Act Out?
It's the time of day when the status gap between teacher and
child is at its greatest. Teacher power is at its height, as you
assume the sacred role of calling the names; child power is at
its lowest, as they sit passively waiting for their turn to respond.
When they act out registration time, they are trying to feel some
of that "teacher power" for themselves.

Of course, we need to establish ourselves as the powerful people in the classroom. We are outnumbered. If they did the maths, we'd be stuffed. But when you want them to look to one another, and not to you, for responses to what they have said, then the status you have built up works against you.

If You Want Children to Be More You Have to Be Less
It's not enough for you to do less during the times when you are encouraging independent learning and thinking: you have to *be* less as well. Make your presence less felt, let go of some control, cease to be the main judge and audience of the talk.

Take a Back Seat is the most important of the Philosophy Circles principles, and is the goal of the other two. The point of Get Moving is to relax the children and get them engaged in one another's answers for the sake of play and sociability, not because you are asking them. The point of using Y-Questions rather than questions with more definitive answers is that they feel that whatever they have to say is as valid as long as they can support it - it is not about finding the answer the teacher wants.

Of Course There Are Times Not to Take a Back Seat
Across the curriculum, adults often have to impart expertise didactically, and it can be painfully inefficient to teach some topics in any other way. Even in a Philosophy Circles session, someone may say something that contains factual misinformation that you feel should be corrected, or on very rare occasions a point can be made that is offensive, breaks school rules, or puts an individual child under unfair attention. You don't cease to be responsible for their welfare while you are facilitating, but the more you can use the techniques in this section to fade into the background, the better.

Go into Orbit

"I Sit in the Circle Just Like the Kids"

The idea that you can be just another person in the circle is "for the birds". It might not be complimentary to say it, but you weigh as much as half your class - in terms of how attention gravitates towards you. So when you sit in the same circle, which seems to be very democratic, the whole circle still tilts towards you. Even when children are doing most of the talking, they will keep looking back to you to find out if what they have said is any good. If you are still controlling the traffic, they have to look at you to find out who gets to speak next.

Always Go into Orbit and facilitate from outside

If the children are in a circle, sit outside it. If they are in rows, get them to face one another and sit in the "Speaker's Chair" position. If they are stood up, hide behind one of the groups so that they talk to one another, not to you.

If more drastic action is needed to stop the children looking at you to direct things, step into a cupboard. Or do what I often do when working with 3-5 year olds: lie down outside the circle, and then pop up like a meerkat when you need to speak.

Help them facilitate themselves

The beginning of this is to hand over control for who speaks to them. Either give them an object to pass round, get each speaker to name the next, or for ruthess efficiency if time is short, get one of the children to choose who speaks next.

It can be hard at first

You feel lazy. You feel you should be giving praise. You feel it's slow because they dither about whose turn it is to speak. But if you have any doubts about making the change, use a **chess clock app** to monitor how much less you talk, and how much more time there is for their voices instead.

> "Initially, the children tended to direct their responses towards the adult. After a couple of weeks however, they were looking at the child they were responding to and dialogue bounced around the room without adult intervention."
>
> Sharree Johnson
> Amesbury Primary School

Scribe, Don't Script!

I was booked to run an INSET by a headteacher who had been doing P4C longer than me. She said it was more credible coming from someone else. I wanted to show off my expertise, so I was ready to fill the slightest pause with some clever facilitation trick.

At the end of the enquiry, the head I had so wanted to impress said, "I think you over-facilitated that. You left no room for us."

There's teaching, and there's "performing" being a teacher
Whenever you teach, you are also performing the role of being a teacher - trying to appear as you feel a teacher should. That means being in control, children doing as you say, reaching the learning objectives. The more eyes that are on you, the more pressure you feel, the more you "perform". Observations, and visitors bring this out in many of us. Even when no other adults are in the room, you are always observing yourself.

I had been "performing" my role as a teacher-trainer. I had a "script" in my head for what I might do, and because of that I was waiting for a pause or a repetition to cue me in, rather than listening deeply for the opportunities in what was being said.

So don't have a script
The children can only fill the space that you give them. Because it goes against your sense of responsibility as a teacher not to have a plan, the temptation is to have a powerpoint with multiple stimuli and questions. But do that, and you'll be thinking about what you are going to do next, not listening as intently to what the children are saying right now.

Scribe to make yourself say less

Writing down reminders of what the children say focuses you on listening. It occupies you, delaying your interventions. Lastly, it makes you unavailable: you're busy writing, so they look to one another, not you, for feedback, giving you less reason to speak.

Scribe so that they drive the direction of the discussion

While you are writing and not talking, they are driving the discussion. Then, when you do intervene, you can use your notes to reflect their thinking back to them, highlighting interesting aspects - so that what you say comes from them, not the other way round, so it is still their words that are deciding the direction.

Often, you will highlight disagreements that have arisen, or invite further comment on emerging Y-Questions, perhaps presenting the options as a Thinkers' Game - "Stand over here if you agree with Grace that... or over here if you agree with Ali that..."

Or you might quote someone to create a speaking frame to help others give their thoughts clearer structure :" John said, 'I think lying is only acceptable if it's to keep you safe.' Does anyone have a different thought like, 'lying is only acceptable if...'?"

Plan The Starts, Not The Endings

Of course, it's nerve-wracking to let go of control and throw away the script. But trust a good stimulus and a compelling question, and stop your planning there. Your learning objective is that they develop the skills needed for independent, intelligent, creative, conceptual conversation. That gives them the tantalizing possibility of taking things in an unexpected direction - remember the pirate mutiny!

Use Their Questions

Most of education, it has been said, is getting children to give other people's answers to other people's questions. That's why the traditional P4C method is perhaps the ultimate way to Take a Back Seat: get children to create their own questions in response to a stimulus and then vote for one to discuss. If you use their questions, not yours, they are in the driving seat from the start.

However, it isn't easy for children who are new to philosophy to come up with conceptually rich questions which will sustain a discussion. Children creating and voting for questions often comes too early - both within a session and in the process of introducing a new group to P4C. The result is that the facilitator sometimes becomes a back seat driver - going along with an unpromising question, but then artificially grafting some philosophical interest onto it by intervening in the discussion.

Their questions can come later in the process
Rather than asking children for questions near the start of a session, when they have only just seen a stimulus, you can ask later on once they have had a substantial discussion - or even at the end, to provide a starting point for the next session. There's usually no need for a formal voting process - one question out of three or four volunteered will probably excite obvious interest and then you can get a consensus to focus on that.

You can also place question creation later in the development of the group. Start by giving them a question, then next time a choice of questions, then inviting them to add to the choices.

Their questions can emerge organically

Sometimes a child will just come out with a question during an enquiry, and that can be a suitable moment for you to pause and refocus the discussion around their question. If their question creates a ripple of reaction and everyone starts talking about it, go with it.

Opinions into questions

You can get a similar ripple of reactions from an opinion that is voiced in the course of the discussion. If a point is made, and everyone immediately starts talking about it, offer the question of whether or not people agree with it. It's you doing the asking, but it's still their question because the impetus comes directly from something that has just been said. Or you might refer to the notes you have been scribing.

Examples into questions

Sometimes a question that is more specific can be more accessible and interesting. For example, if free range chickens are mentioned in a discussion about whether animals have rights, narrow the focus to that single species. Or sometimes, take the opposite approach and increase the scope of a question, asking if the reasons given in an example apply to all similar situations, to raise the discussion to a more conceptual level.

Questions into stimuli or discussions

An excellent use of their questions is when a child asks a question at some other time in the week and you find a stimulus that will help the whole class to discuss it. Or best of all, if just as you are about to start, someone asks a question, others react, and you are willing to Take a Back Seat altogether and see what emerges!

Take a Back Seat

Summary

In facilitating P4C, your "teacher power" works against you

Make yourself small, invisible, unavailable

They can only fill the space you leave them

Focus on listening to them, not "performing" the role of teacher.

Be the servant, not the boss

Go into Orbit

Physically remove yourself from the circle

Delegate responsibility for choosing who speaks

Resist the temptation to praise

Scribe, Don't Script!

Let them drive the direction of the discussion

Scribe down what they say so you can reflect it back to them

Plan the starts, not the ends

Use Their Questions

Questions don't have to be created near the beginning

Turn opinions and examples into questions

Be willing to drop your questions in favour of theirs

About the Authors

Jason Buckley is the founder of The Philosophy Man. He has practiced P4C with thousands of participants, from nursery age through to undergraduates and teachers.

He is also Director of Studies at GIFT, the UK's leading provider of enrichment courses for the most able children, and founder of Outspark, which runs DofE Expeditions. He lives on a narrowboat and enjoys caving and musical comedy improv.

Tom Bigglestone is Lead Trainer at The Philosophy Man. A former Head of Religious Studies and teacher of more subjects than he can remember, he now trains teachers in P4C and enjoys working with pupils week-in, week-out. He curates the bulletin, which is received by over 16,000 teachers, specialising in finding opportunities for philosophy in the curriculum. Tom is also particularly interested in how progress can be assessed in philosophy - the subject of his research for the Walter Hines-Page Scholarship in 2014.